HEAD
OVER
HEELS

TATENDA DUNE

Head Over Heels
Copyright © 2019 Munaii Bookworks.

All rights reserved. No portion of this book may be reproduced, stored in a retrieval system, or transmitted in any form or by any means electronic, mechanical, photocopy, recording, scanning, or other, except for brief quotations in critical reviews or articles, or as specifically allowed by the U. S. Copyright Act of 1976, as amended, without the prior written permission of the publisher.

Published by Munaii Bookworks

Unless otherwise noted, Scripture quotations are from the Holy Bible, New International Version (NIV). Copyright © 1973, 1978, 1984, 2011. International Bible Society. Used by permission of Zondervan Bible Publishers.

Quotations designed KJV are from the King James Version. Public domain.

Quotations designated NASB are from the NEW AMERICAN STANDARD BIBLE, © 1960, 1962, 1963, 1968, 1971, 1972, 1973, 1975, 1977, 1995 by The Lockman Foundation. Used by permission.
Quotations designated NLT are from the *Holy Bible*, New Living Translation, copyright © 1996, 2004. Used by permission of Tyndale House Publishers, Inc., Carol Stream, Illinois 60188. All rights reserved.
Poem printed with permission by Bethany Dunn ISBN-13: 978-0-9861018-8-5

Printed in the United States of America

To all my single sisters

⁴*God* is patient and kind; *God* does not envy or boast; *He* is not arrogant ⁵or rude. *He* does not insist on his own way; *He* is not irritable or resentful; ⁶*He* does not rejoice at wrongdoing but rejoices with the truth. ⁷*Jesus* bears all things, believes all things, hopes all things, endures all things. ⁸*Jesus* never ends. As for prophecies, they will pass away; as for tongues, they will cease; as for knowledge, it will pass away. ⁹For we know in part and we prophesy in part, ¹⁰but when *HE* comes, the partial will pass away. ¹¹When I was a child, I spoke like a child, I thought like a child, I reasoned like a child. When I became a man, I gave up childish ways. ¹²For now we see in a mirror dimly, but then face to face. Now I know in part; then I shall know fully, even as I have been fully known. ¹³So now faith, hope, and love abide, these three; but the greatest of these is *God (love)*.

1 Corinthians 13 New International Version (NIV), *emphasis mine*

Contents

Introduction vii
    Chapter 1: Awakening... 1
    Chapter 2: He Loves You 4
    Chapter 3: First Love 6
    Chapter 4: He Comes to Steal, Kill, and Destroy 11
    Chapter 5: The Escape 23
    Chapter 6: Where Does It Hurt? 27
    Chapter 7: Sex, Love, and Marriage 38
    Chapter 8: Let Him In 49
Conclusion.. 53
The Divine Dance 65
Acknowledgments 67
About the Author 70
Journal 71

Introduction

*Love the Lord your God with all your heart
and with all your soul and with all your mind.
Matthew 22:37*

Until I was in my mid-twenties, I had never walked into a church and listened to the preacher talk about how so in love he/she was with Jesus and how Jesus felt the same. I have always heard and read that Jesus loves us but never that he is *in* love with us. Considering how love is depicted in the world today, I think that might have to do with a misunderstanding of what being "in love" means. Nevertheless, this is a subject that is rarely taught and needs to be addressed.

I have gotten various reactions from people when I told them about the concept of this book. There are some who just nodded and pretended I never said anything. Others looked at me as if I was out of my mind. A few inquired about how long the book was and thought it was an exciting subject. Even fewer people asked for a more detailed explanation of what I meant by being in love with Jesus.

Dear sister, God loves you more than you can ever imagine! And the purpose of this book is to help you begin to understand his great love for you. It is time that the church learns to fall in love with the one who has loved us with an everlasting love. Jesus' love for us is more than a generic love he has for everyone; it is personal. He loves you as if you are the only person in the world. He loves you deeply and with such great passion that it is hard to fathom, but he wants you to let yourself receive it because only then will you begin to fall in love with him too. My message is specifically for single women because I know many of you seek completeness from relationships with men, and my goal is to help you redirect your focus from men to Jesus: the only Man who can genuinely complete you.

As you read each page in this book, I pray that you open your heart and receive whatever the Holy Spirit says to you. You will not regret it.

Chapter 1

Awakening

*Let the king be enthralled by your beauty;
honor him, for he is your lord.
Psalm 45:11*

One time there was a guy who was relentlessly pursuing me.

For a time, I did not know it, but he would find different ways to let me know just how much he wanted me. He never stopped coming after me, but he was and still is, crazily in love with me. Of course, I did not know he was really *after* me. The two of us would spend time together almost every day, and though I missed the loving gazes he would give me, the sweet words he sometimes whispered, and the lavish gifts he gave me, I failed to use. I was interested in someone else. Really, I was interested in every other guy but him, yet none of those men ever gave me the time of day. There was always someone more stunning than I, and they always chose the pretty, little, skinny... yeah, there was always someone else.

Then one day I gave up chasing men who did not want me. I quit. And that was when this guy said something I had never heard him say before. He held my hand, looked me in the eyes, and said, "I am enthralled by your beauty." A few days later, I recalled that moment as it opened my heart to the melting love of my true lover, my Savior, my King, and my God, Jesus Christ.

I was in my third year at Texas A&M University and I was still on my quest to find a boyfriend. Since I stopped thinking boys were gross, every boy I had ever liked always seemed to like someone else. You can imagine how much damage I allowed that to do to my self-esteem. During that third year in university, I started liking a particular guy. I did everything I knew to do to get his attention, but to no avail. Every time I saw him, I would hug him, and I would make sure we had a lengthy conversation. I would dress better in hopes of getting at least one compliment from him, but he never gave me the attention I craved. Finally, after months of being infatuated with him, I came to my senses and realized that he and I were nothing close to compatible. I recognized that we would never be together, and I would have been miserable if by some miracle we dated, so I stopped the pursuit.

A week or two after I gave up pursuing him, I visited my friend Whitney's church. During the worship, I said to myself, "I give up chasing boys," and immediately I had a vision of myself in front of God's throne with my arms spread wide. I could not see him, but I said to him, "I'm all yours, God. I'm all yours."

At that moment, Whitney, who was standing next to me, dropped down, got her Bible, read a verse, and then turned to me and said the Lord had just given her a word for me. That word was Psalm 45:11, which says, "The king is enthralled by your beauty; honor him, for he is your lord." She then proceeded to tell me that not only did Jesus love everyone, but he loved me specially. She made it personal. She said Jesus *was* and *is* in love with me. She continued talking, but at that point, I was hardly paying attention to her. My mind was still trying to process that the King did not just think I was beautiful, but he was awed by my beauty. I amazed him. I captivated him. The Almighty God in all his glory and majesty was enchanted, mesmerized, and entranced by me. That alone was enough to tap into places in my heart that had long been hardened by all the pain I had experienced over my life, and it took me over a year to fully receive that truth.

Chapter 2

He Loves You

*Jesus loves me, this I know,
for the Bible tells me so.*

What a wonderful truth and song that is, but do you really *know* that it is true? Do you believe it? What exactly does it mean for him to love you? Take a second and think about those questions.

Chances are, even though you just read the previous chapter, you may have come up with the stereotypical pulpit answers, such as, "God loves me so much that he was willing to sacrifice his Son, so I could be redeemed and have eternal life with him." Or, "God loves me because he created me, and he loves all of his creation." Or maybe, "God loves me because he made me in his image; Jesus loves me because he says so somewhere in the Bible, and God does not lie, so yeah, I guess he does."

Although all of these answers are true, many people fail to understand how *much* God loves us. In truth, as long as we are on this side of heaven, we are never going to fully comprehend how deep his love is for us. Nonetheless, the beauty of the Christian life is this: throughout your walk, Jesus will continually reveal more of his love to you, if you will let him. That is the key; you have to allow him to show himself to you because he will not impose himself on you. However, I have realized that many Christians do not ask for the revelation of his great love because of how generalized they view God's love, and you may be part of that group. After all, the Bible says, "For God so loved the *world*"(John 3:16, emphasis mine), not a specific person. So, whether or not you are aware of it, you have deduced that that's as much love as you are going to get from him.

Yes, Jesus loves everyone, but *everyone* is comprised of individuals, and you are an individual. He loves *you*, specifically. When he was beaten and hung on the cross, he was thinking about you. As he experienced the wrath of God, the chastisement of *all your* sins, he was looking forward to spending eternity with you. He sacrificed himself for you so that you would never have to experience what you truly deserved. He is crazy for you! There is a place in his heart that only you can fill, and he longs for you to fill it.

Dear sister, Jesus is madly in love with you! He longs for your time. He wants you to spend your days in his presence where he can woo you and whisper sweet words into your heart. He longs for your heart. He wants you to open every part of yourself to him freely; he longs for you to let him enter those painful, fragile parts of you and caress your throbbing heart. He longs to give you the peace that only comes from surrendering everything to him. He longs to see you smile and see your eyes twinkle at the thought of him because he is absolutely, marvelously, wholeheartedly captivated by you, and he wants you to feel the same about him. He loves you. Do not worry about everyone else; they are his problem. He loves *you*.

Chapter 3

First Love

*The Lord appeared to us in the past, saying:
"I have loved you with an everlasting love."
Jeremiah 31:3*

"You can never forget your first love." I cannot tell you how many times I have heard women say that in movies and on TV, and for a long time I thought I had to lose a first love before I could get married. That's how it goes, right? You fall in love, you and your lover fall apart, you find someone else, you get married, then one day, *dans un petit café à Paris,* you bump into your first love again. You cheat on your current husband; ahem, excuse me. You passionately rekindle your flame (cheater!!) in the most luxurious suite of the Hotel Plaza Athena with a beautiful view of the Eiffel Tower. The two of you realize that you married the wrong people, so you divorce your spouses, marry each other, and live happily ever after!

Or you never rekindle the flame you once had with your first love, but luckily you found someone else. Nevertheless, when the moon is high, the night is still, and you slowly drift into a sweet slumber, you see your first love's face. You dream of the love you shared only to wake up to your second, third, maybe fourth love's side, and you sigh thinking of what you once had.

Okay, so maybe I went a little too far with the scenario, but you get the point. Society has told us that we never forget our first loves. In fact, you may be thinking about him right now. Sadly, woman of God, the man or boy you are thinking about right now is *not* your first love. And for those like me who do not have the supposed *obligatory* first love, even you have forgotten your first love.

When God created mankind, He planned on having a deep and intimate relationship with his creation. For example, if you read the book of Genesis, you will see that Adam walked closely with God (Genesis 2:16-17 – God gives a command to Adam, Genesis 3:8 – Adam and Eve hear God walking in the garden). How else could he have named all of the animals of the world and have everything he ever needed to live in the garden without a close relationship with his Maker? God loved Adam, and Adam loved God. We can say the same of Eve because she too was God's creation. However, when the two decided to sin against God, they walked away from their Lover and right into the arms of the enemy. They let themselves be seduced by what Satan had to offer - death disguised as God's ploy to deprive them of goodness. They forgot everything God had for them and who he was to them. You have likely done the same.

At this point, I hope it is obvious to you that God is not calling you to love him as you love your aunt or your mother or brother. He wants you to love him as a lover, a fiancé, a husband.

That is the most intimate type of love, and that is what he wants from you. However, the problem may be that you keep running away from him. You have abandoned your first love, and to fill that part of you that only Jesus can fill, you are dating lots of men and obsessing over which one is "the one," instead of running to the One.

Or maybe your search for a man has been futile. No guy has ever asked you out. Perhaps there are some who showed interest, but they were good for nothing, jobless, one-track-minded scoundrels with crooked teeth and no swag, so now you feel inadequate because there seems to be no *good* man out there who wants you.

Or maybe the men you like always overlook you and pick your friends, so now you feel ugly and unwanted. However, instead of going to the One who has loved you with an everlasting love for comfort, you have let yourself be deceived by the one who hates you and wants to destroy you.

A Quick Story

I used to have a roommate who thought she trusted God to find her a husband. However, she often went on dates in hopes of finding her life partner only to be disappointed when nothing came out of her attempts to locate him. She believed that it was important to be open and direct with men and to go on dates with them in order to learn more about them before making a decision whether or not she'll let them court her. I told her I would rather not waste time and money on a date but ask the Holy Spirit to tell me what I need to know from the get-go. She wished God would do the same with her, but she never invited him into that conversation. Many times, she asked me to pray for the men in whom she was interested and here is how I would pray:

Me: Daddy, what's up with this one?
God: He's a waste of time.
Me: Okay. Does she know that? God: No.

After the joy of talking to a possible mate would eventually subside or the men ended up not being what she expected, she would be disappointed and find fault in them. I would be tempted to tell her to just ask God instead of going on all her dates, but I could tell she enjoyed the chase more than she wished to truly hear what God would say.

There was a time she spent a couple of hours preparing herself for dinner with a gentleman who was several years older than her. After she finished, the Holy Spirit told me that it would not end well with this man. Right before she left for dinner, she jokingly complained about how it takes a long time for a woman to dress for a date, but then admitted that she enjoyed the preparation and the anticipation of an exciting time. At that moment, I felt that she had not prepared herself spiritually for this date, so I inquired if she had prayed for herself and this gentleman to which she responded with this sarcastic remark, "Oh yeah, that" and walked out the door. It had never crossed her mind to let God speak to her about this date. And judging from her response and immediate departure, she didn't intend to ask.

Ladies, if this is how you treat God when it comes to your love life, you're setting yourself up for heartbreak. The dinner date went well, and she was happy, but God had shown me through a vision that he had claimed her heart for himself. He said until she completely surrenders her love life to him, she will continue to go on pointless dates and be disappointed over and over again. She and the young man set up another date, but he canceled it at the last minute and gave her a mediocre excuse. He promised to make up for it later, but then one day, after ignoring her text messages and neglecting all communication for days, he told her the truth: he wasn't interested anymore. She, in turn, placed all the blame on him and wished he had told her that in the beginning when in truth she should have asked God for his opinion. If so, she would have saved herself three weeks of emotional turmoil and relieved me of hearing all about it.

Chapter 4

He Comes to Steal, Kill, and Destroy

He prowls around like a roaring lion, looking for someone to devour.
1 Peter 5:8 NLT

The devil hates you. Do not for any reason believe that, "He is not that bad." He is *worse* than you think or imagine. He is the cause of every single negative situation you have ever faced in your life: disease, poverty, heartbreak, strife, etc. He is a liar, a thief, and a destroyer (see John 10:10). Jesus describes Satan as the "father of all lies" (John 8:44). Lying is his nature, and he knows nothing else. He uses his native tongue, lying, to destroy you. He does not want to see you prosper. He wants you to suffer. He hates you. He despises you. He is seething with anger towards you and is determined to make you a miserable piece of rubbish so that he can laugh at you when he has led you down his destructive path. That is his main task in this world; crush everyone, keep them from God, deceive them all their lives, and hope they die before they are saved so that they can be tormented with him when his day finally comes.

The Hunt

Before I move on, I would like to share my testimony with you. As much as I would rather not share some details of my life, it is absolutely imperative that I be authentic so that you can see how horrible the devil is, how Jesus worked in my life to get me to a point where I can wholeheartedly say that I am in love with him, and how you can do it too.

I was born and raised in Harare, Zimbabwe, and like many young girls there, I grew up going to church. It was not an option *not* to go to church on Sundays, so every Sunday, I went to the services with my mother. I loved it. The music was great, but the food after the service was even better. By the time I was eight years old, I had memorized three verses, and Jesus had visited me in a dream once, so there was no doubt in my mind that he existed and that he loved me.

However, by that same time, the devil was already at work. I found myself, at eight years, old feeling as though I was not good enough for anyone. Little boys I had liked never seemed to like me back. My father was hardly involved in my life; I felt like an outcast every time I visited him and his side of the family. As I grew older and watched television and listened to the hit music of the day, what I saw and heard further emphasized my feelings of worthlessness. I found out that I did not have the right skin color, the right nationality, or the right weight. I was not limber enough, easy enough, rich enough, and the list goes on.

To make matters worse, I moved to the US at age eleven (my mom had moved there two years earlier), and the students at my junior high school made me feel as if I was half a person because I was African. They thought I was stupid and could not speak English, so they would talk negatively about me in my presence (even after they realized I understood every single word they said). They made fun of my accent, my choice of words (I spoke British English), my hair, and my background. Most of them did not believe I had flown to America; they thought I had come by swimming or on a raft. They assumed that in Zimbabwe, there were no modern advances whatsoever, so they thought I used to live in a mud hut, walked around naked, and that I used to hunt for a living. Every time I tried to correct their prejudice, I was deemed a liar, and they mocked and bullied me even more. I hated living in America, and I wanted to go back home.

Besides, I was also very lonely. Among the Zimbabweans living in the Dallas, Texas area at that time, I was the only one in my age group, so there was no one with whom I could relate my struggles. There was a Sudanese girl at my school whom I befriended, but I never got close to her. I projected the feelings I had about myself onto her and that hindered our friendship from developing well. There was a time I tried to confide in my mother, but the way she responded to my vulnerability caused me to withdraw from her emotionally. She would, "Toughen up. That's how life is in America." With all of this happening, I had to adjust to my new life and find a way to cope.

I turned to my imagination. In my mind, I was everything I thought I should be in order to be happy, and most times I played out that ideal Tatenda in the MSN Games chat rooms (a/s/l anyone?). In those chat rooms, I was the perfected version of myself. I was a white sixteen-year-old girl (by this time I was twelve) living in Los Angeles, California. I had many highly attractive male friends with whom I was a little too promiscuous. I drove a Jeep (shout out to my girl Tina!), and I had all the cool friends in school, just as in the movies. I would private chat with many guys (Lord knows how old those people really were) and imagine myself having sex with them as we exchanged very sexual words with each other. They would ask me what I was wearing, and I would lie and describe the best type of lingerie I could conjure up. Some wanted to know where I lived so they could come to visit me, but dumb as I was, I was still clever enough to never reveal that information. I did this for several months until the devil, or whatever evil spirit was working in my life, decided he wanted to drag me deeper into my misery.

One day, I was chatting with two people when one of them asked me if I was *horny*. I had no idea what that was, so the person gave me a website and told me that I would find out what that word meant if I visited the website. I foolishly went on the website, and that ill-fated moment began my seven-year addiction to pornography. Yes, for those of you who are already judging, females struggle with that too.

I started viewing pictures and watching short clips on the website, but soon that did not satisfy my desire, so I found other websites and signed up for email subscriptions. The addiction escalated so rapidly that, at one point, I nearly committed credit card fraud just so I could have more access to videos online since the free content did not show much. About a year later, I cried out to God for help because there were many pop-up ads for porn websites on the computer, and my mother was wondering how that was happening. (Luckily for me, she did not know much about computers to know that someone had probably been going on pornography websites for there to be those kinds of pop-ups.) The morning after I had prayed to God for help, the computer crashed. I was not too happy about that, but that was how God chose to fix the issue, so I did not argue.

A few months later, we moved to another city, and I had no recollection of ever watching porn. We got a new computer, and I had nothing to do online except to check my email (I had started using MSN instead of my Yahoo account (the one where all the porn newsletters were sent) and play games on the Disney Channel and The-N (now called Teen Nick) websites. Not once did I think to go on MSN Games or porn websites as I had previously done.

One day, however, I was channel-surfing around midnight, and I came across a porno on one of the premium movie channels on cable, and I suddenly remembered that I used to watch porn, so I relapsed. Every weekend, I would stay up and wait for my mother to go to bed so I could watch freely in the living room. Unfortunately, my mother would periodically get up and pass by the living room on her way to the bathroom, so to avoid being caught, I asked her to get me my own television. That way I could watch in my room every night without her disturbing me. In time, just like any addiction, I built up a tolerance. I needed more than the soft porn on TV to satisfy me.

I quickly moved on to downloading hardcore movies to the new computer, but after a few months, that did not gratify the lust that had overtaken me either, so I moved on to masturbating while watching, and I eventually developed a really dirty mind. I would spend hours fantasizing, and that began to take a toll on me. I would be in class, and I would miss major parts of lessons or lose time on my exams because my mind kept on drifting. Over time, I ended up masturbating and fantasizing at the same time in order to gratify the desire. (I figured out how to do it in public without anyone knowing what was happening.) At that point, the only thing left was to have sex.

Glory be to God, five years into my addiction I got saved. It happened the summer after I graduated from high school. During my senior year, I had been going to a Bible study at my school, and people there kept talking about salvation, so I got curious. I never asked anyone what it meant, but I kept on asking myself what it was. One day, while I was watching a girl worshipping during the worship portion of the Bible study, I saw something in her that made me think, "She has something that I don't have, and whatever it is, I want it."

After that, I borrowed the book *Jesus Freaks* by D.C. Talk (a collection of stories about martyrs) from one of the girls in the study, and while reading the book, I asked myself what it was about Jesus that people were willing to die for him. Later, after reading about a martyr who had a vision of herself going to heaven, I told myself that I wanted to go to heaven too, and I asked God what I needed to do to get there. Since no one ever witnessed to me during the school year, my questions were left unanswered. Fortunately, during the summer, I borrowed the album, *United We Stand,* by Hillsong United from a family friend, and after listening to it all day, I accepted Jesus as my Lord and Savior.

That was the best feeling I have ever had in my life! When Jesus entered my heart, I felt so loved and overwhelmed that I did not know what to do. I wanted to jump around and shout for joy, but my mother was in the living room with me (she had no idea what was going on), and I did not want her thinking I had gone nuts, so I wrote a song instead. As I was writing, I saw something twinkling in the room, and I knew my mother and I were not the only ones in the room. I could almost see the angels rejoicing with me.

Summer holiday ended and I went to university. I was excited to begin a new life, and I had a sense of confidence that I did not understand. I did not want to watch porn anymore or think about all sorts of raunchy acts I could do with a guy, but I was still me. Although I had been saved, I still struggled with most of my issues. Even though I pretended the issues were resolved and everything was fine, the way my schoolmates in junior high had treated me had made a deep impact on my self-worth. I was ashamed of my background and my ethnicity, and I was still insecure. That year, I lived in the dorm with a gorgeous roommate whose lifestyle I envied. She went out all the time, had money to burn and had nice clothes and many friends (some of them admittedly promiscuous). She did things I wished I could do with a few basketball players, and that brought all my problems to the surface, so I fell into the same destructive pattern again.

A Brief Rant

It infuriates me how sin is categorized! Who is the idiot who said that certain sexual sins belong to men and others to women? Because of that categorization, for two and a half years into my salvation, I believed that my struggles were abnormal for a woman. I felt that I could not confide in anyone because among many of the believers whom I trusted, there was a sense that only men struggled with porn, masturbation, and graphic fantasies, whereas women struggled with promiscuity, prostitution, flowery fantasies, or better yet, they did not struggle with sexual immorality at all!

I Corinthians 6: 16-20

[16] And don't you realize that if a man joins himself to a prostitute, he becomes one body with her? For the Scriptures say, "The two are united into one."[a] [17] But the person who is joined to the Lord is one spirit with him.

[18] Run from sexual sin! No other sin so clearly affects the body as this one does. For sexual immorality is a sin against your own body. [19] Don't you realize that your body is the temple of the Holy Spirit, who lives in you and was given to you by God? You do not belong to yourself,[20] for God bought you with a high price. So you must honor God with your body. (NLT)

Last time I checked, the devil works in everyone, male and female! He does not categorize his attacks based on gender; he attacks where there is opportunity.

Fortunately, now that I was saved, the Lord would convict me of my righteousness. I knew better than to watch porn or fantasize for hours, but it was extremely difficult to stop. I tried. I had memorized what my friend Amy called "a butt-kicking verse" (I Corinthians 6:18–20) that I sometimes read to help me stay away from the porn, and the times I read it or meditated on it were helpful. At times, however, the temptation was too great, so I would end up giving in before I remembered to read or meditate on the verse.

Eventually, I desperately wanted to tell someone about my problem because keeping it a secret made me feel worse about myself. However, every time I heard someone testify about his porn addiction, he would always say porn is a male problem. Even the media and many Christians believe it is only a male problem, so I would sit there and think, "But I'm female." I felt alone. The shame and guilt intensified so much that I wished I was a slut because that seemed to be a more *appropriate* sexual sin for a Christian woman. So, for nearly three years, I did not tell anyone. In June 2009, the summer before my third year in college, I decided I was done being a Christian because nothing good seemed to be coming out of it. I felt that Christianity was all work with no reward. I had been reading my Bible, going to church, praising and praying to this God who seemed disinterested in making my life any better, so I quit. I decided I was going to do exactly what I wanted, so I spent three days watching pornography on my laptop. I would wake up, eat, watch porn, eat some more, watch more porn, shower, and then sleep. On the third night, I had a moment of clarity and it dawned on me that I had been watching porn for three days. I was shocked. I told God that if these three days were an example of how the rest of my life would be without him, then the porn had to go, and it did. I instantly lost all the desire to watch it, and my mind was at its clearest for the first time in seven years. I looked back over my life, and I could not believe that I had spent seven years watching pornography. Although the porn addiction ended, the fantasies continued. They were less graphic, but still bothersome. It was not until December 2011 that they completely stopped.

At a women's retreat at my church in February of 2010, I was finally able to confess my sin. I had attended a session called "The Secret Life" in which the speaker challenged all of us to tell someone the "one secret we would rather take to the grave than admit." She listed some secrets that we probably had, and to my surprise, she mentioned pornography. She said that confessing our sins would free us from the guilt and the shame, so even though I was afraid, I confessed to two lovely ladies who were in my small group at the church and who had also attended the same session. Ever since then, I have been free of the guilt and shame, and most importantly, the sin into which I had foolishly dug and burrowed myself. I was finally in a position in which God could deal with the issues that had led me to pornography. I was surrounded by women in my church with whom I could talk whenever my thoughts went astray. This allowed for healing to continue and the accountability helped me to keep away the desire to watch pornography.

A few months later, I visited Whitney's church, that friend God spoke to at the same time he spoke to me. My heart had been softened enough and strongholds had been broken such that I could now receive the revelation that Jesus was in love with me and not reject it. When Whitney shared this revelation with me, together with Psalm 45:11, I didn't know what to do with it. What is a woman to do when she finds out the king of this universe is awestruck by her? I felt bad for not responding to God or Whitney. So, four days later, I sent her a message and told her what had been going on. My mind was still trying to understand why Jesus would love me like that.

After this encounter with Jesus, he withdrew and was silent. He switched from wooing me to fixing the heart issues that had drawn me away from him. This process was frustrating and painful, but freeing. The main problem had been the emotional turmoil that had come from my father's rejection and abandonment. During another retreat the following year, God helped me see that I equated Abba, Father to my earthly father. I had a difficult time comprehending God loving me as daddy. I didn't know what that looked like. He also began to re-form my identity. During my last year in school, I felt as if he separated me mentally from parental influence in order for me to see him clearly. He wanted to show me what *he* said about me. He then returned to teaching me to love him as a lover. During the summer after I graduated from university, I found myself longing for Jesus. I missed him and I yearned to be held in his arms and rest my head on his chest.

When I look back to this time period, I see that God was working on my maturity and he continues to do so in many ways. Although I was 21 and at an age where most young adults in America are ready to enter the working world as professionals, I still behaved like an adolescent. I didn't know myself. I was financially inept. I expected others to take care of me and direct me. I didn't know what I wanted with my life. I had an extremely tainted physical view of myself, and I held a strong belief that I was unworthy to be loved by anybody. I was too proud of how spiritual I was, and I used my spirituality to cover up my inadequacies. Regardless, I was starting to discover myself a little bit more.

In August of 2011, I returned home from college. I had graduated and was not sure of my future path, so I stayed with my mother. In September, she left for vacation and I was faced with three choices during her absence. I could spend my free time watching television, watching porn on the internet, or relaxing with the Holy Spirit. I chose the latter.

For nearly six weeks, I could not stop thinking about Jesus. I talked to him *all* the time; in the shower, at work, while I was driving, while cooking, and the like. I would fall asleep talking to him, and when I woke up my first thought was, "I love you, Jesus," and then I would pick up the conversation where I had left it. I did not want to do anything but worship him. I hardly watched the television or listened to anything other than Christian music. I would shuffle all my Christian stations on Pandora and play them for hours. I would go on long walks after church every Sunday and talk to him about the sermon and everything I was looking forward to once I got to heaven. I wished I could physically see him and touch him, and I was delighted when he told me he wished I could see him and touch him too. I hardly slept at night because I would spend hours praying. I wanted nothing else, but to be totally consumed by his presence. Simply put, I was madly in love and am still in love with him.

Chapter 5

The Escape

*He said to me, "My grace is sufficient for you,
for my power is made perfect in weakness."
2 Corinthians 12:9*

However, as the lover of my soul whispered sweet words in my ear, the enemy was lurking in the shadows seeking to destroy the seeds God was planting. Although I spent a marvelous six weeks dancing to the whispers of my lover, Satan was waiting for his opportunity to strike. He stood by with a record of all my wrong doings and broken promises and replayed them. To my dismay, I found myself reverting to old habits – negative thoughts about my life, my family, and seeking to appease God by striving to get his love and attention. I thought I wasn't good enough for him anymore; that I wasn't pleasing to him. My thoughts went astray again, and I started fantasizing as a crutch. Thankfully, the fantasies lasted but a few days. I asked God to help me clear my thoughts and he did, but I was still striving to please him. I had forgotten who I was again – the beloved daughter of Jehovah Elohim.

Fortunately, I was quick to run to him this time, and in turn, he taught me who he was and who I am through the teachings of Dr. Creflo Dollar in College Park, Georgia. Everything the Holy Spirit had taught me during the six weeks I spent enamored by him came to life again as I delved deeper into the Bible and received revelation knowledge about the scriptures I read. I fell in love again, but this time I had a scriptural understanding of my identity in Christ, and I was able to shield myself from the devil's flaming arrows by the power of the spoken word of God. I learned to ground myself in God's word. The enemy had tried to entrap me, but my Daddy, God and Savior Jesus released me from his claws and rescued me again. I escaped by turning to God, and you can too.

Earlier I said the devil is out to get you. He wants to steal, kill, and destroy you, and that is why we face so many of the problems we have today. God, in contrast, wants to help you because he loves you. Unfortunately, he is often the last one we turn to for help. I had many problems and I turned to pornography to numb my pain. My question for you is, what have you turned to in order to numb your pain? Where do you go to hide from your struggles? Chances are, you might be depressed and/or suicidal. Maybe you are addicted to something or someone, or perhaps you are involved in activities that are detrimental to your soul and/or your body.

With what have you replaced God? Perhaps you watch pornography as I did. Maybe you have turned to drugs, sex, promiscuity, prostitution (this also includes those who are TATENDA DUNE "actresses" or "models" in the porn industry), masturbation, shopping, exercising, cutting, overworking, gossiping, TV watching, social media, cleaning, hoarding, alcohol, gambling, food (not eating it, or eating too much), criminal behavior, or partying. Maybe you are always angry, filled with hatred, unforgiving, or you are violent. Perhaps you keep yourself busy by volunteering or going to concerts or various sporting events. Possibly you are involved in many organizations, or you play several sports. Maybe you are always doing something, and you purposely never give yourself time to be alone.

You have thought about asking God for help, but you feel ashamed or your addiction/negative behaviors are now holding you captive. You feel guilty. You hear a voice telling you that God does not want to help someone like you; it says he only helps perfect people. It tells you that saved people do not do the things you have done, and they do not have problems as you do. You go to church and the pastor and other church members condemn you. You have tried everything you can to help yourself; counselling, self-help books, or self-restraint strategies, but you always fail. It is time for you to stop trying to overcome these by your own strength and turn to Jesus.

His "grace is sufficient for you" (2 Corinthians 12:9) or his "grace is all you need" (NLT) because he is power. You cannot beat that. He is *the* solution. Do not pay attention to the voice that is telling you God will not help you. Jesus came to the earth for that very purpose - to help you. He was "sent to heal the broken hearted" (Luke 4:18 KJV). That's you, and he wants to set you free from bondage. Let him help you overcome your addiction, your bad behaviors, your negative thoughts, your overly busy life, and then watch the issues that led you to all of those poor choices disappear as well. Ask him for help. He says, "Call upon me in the day of trouble;

I will deliver you, and you will honor me" (Psalm 50:15). He promises to help you, but you have to ask. God is a gentleman; he will not impose himself on you, so do yourself a favor and take refuge in his loving arms. He loves you and is waiting for your call.

Chapter 6

Where Does It Hurt?

*I praise you because I am fearfully and
wonderfully made; Your works are wonderful;
I know that full well.*
Psalm 139:14

Thinking back to my porno-watching days, I now realize that pornography was my escape from my loneliness, an escape from what I had come to believe about myself through those who bullied me as well as other experiences. Instead of running to God to take refuge in him, I sank deeper into deceit, and everything got worse because the devil was playing with me even more. That is exactly where he wants you. He loves tormenting you. He thrives on putting you down, confusing you, beating you, controlling you, lying to you, enticing you, then stabbing you right where it hurts over and over again. He is aroused by your pain, your tears, and your helplessness. He loves it.

Now that you know exactly how the devil feels about you and what he wants to do to you, open your heart, search down deep, and think about the issues in your life that have driven you even further away from God and straight into Satan's claws. Where does it hurt? I am going to discuss some topics to help you in your search. If they do not apply to you, that is okay. Make your own list and let the Holy Spirit guide you in your search. Let him peel away what was never meant for you.

Body Image

What bothers you about your body? Is your hair too thin, too thick, breaking, or graying? Is your tongue too long or too short? Is your nose too wide, too pointed, or too bumpy? Do you have humongous lips, thin lips, large lower/upper lip compared to the other? Are your nostrils too flared or too narrow? Your bottom, is it nonexistent, too big, too flabby, or too dimpled? Do your inner thighs touch? Do you have hairy toes, a hairy bikini line, a hairy chest, or a moustache? Are you too fat or too skinny? Are your feet too large or too small? What is the issue? Do you have birthmarks or freckles? Are your cheekbones not high enough? Are your breasts too small, too big, too saggy, or too perky? Do you have rabbit teeth, crooked teeth, rotten teeth, or missing teeth? I could go on, but you know what bothers you.

Many people have something about their bodies that they do not like. I feel it is worse for women, considering how often we buy the lie that there is such a thing as a perfect body. The media tells us how the "perfect woman" looks. That, by the way, is defined by men. (What do they know about women, anyway?) Are you familiar with 36-24-36? These are the bra, waist, and hip measurements that men supposedly like. It is the hourglass-shaped body that exemplifies a woman who is a "perfect ten" - the one after whom all men supposedly lust. However, since these measurements are not possible for every woman (you have to be a certain height, weight, and have a bone structure that can handle these measurements), now all women are supposed to aspire to look like those air-brushed and photo-shopped stick people on the magazine covers. We all know they look fake, but for some reason, we still strive to attain that "perfect look." I hate to break it to you, ladies, but no matter how much plastic surgery you have, diets you observe, or exercises you do, you will never look like anyone in those magazines. Thanks to the *wonders* of photo editing software; *they* do not even look like their pictures!

Some of you think that by having the perfect body, you will be loved more, treated with more respect, have a better life, and be happier. By doing that, you are looking for acceptance in a harsh and cruel world instead of turning to Jesus for acceptance. He does not judge you based on your looks. He judges you based on who you are - his creation, and he loves you. So, get this in your head: as long as you live on this earth, you will *never* have a perfect body. I know I just crushed some of your hearts, but that is the truth. The good news is - if you accepted Jesus as your Savior, when you get your *resurrected* body, you will be perfect, exactly the way God intended for your body to look. Everything about you will be sensational, brilliant, and magnificent. Right now, you are living in your earthly body. The only part of you that is perfect is your spirit because that is the part of you that is "joined unto the Lord" (1 Corinthians 6:17 KJV). Your soul is still being transformed (Romans 12:2), and your body will be made perfect upon the resurrection of the dead (1 Corinthians 15:40–49).

In the meantime, do not stress over your physical body that is going to be buried once you leave. You are not going to take it with you, so why bother fussing so much over something that is going to decompose once you are gone? That said, you still need to take care of yourself. Keep yourself healthy because your body is God's temple. Let him help you take care of it so that you will be able to function well in this physical world.

Ethnicity

Somehow, we (in this case, women) have been deceived into thinking that we all should look, dress, and act like the type of people we see portrayed in the media. When speaking, we should all sound prim and proper. As far as accents go, we should all sound American or have a British or maybe an Australian accent if you are an English speaker. Maybe you live in a francophone country and you feel the pressure to sound Parisian when speaking French.

I know that some of you may be in disagreement with me on this one, but have you ever questioned why you do the things you do to make yourself look or act "perfect?" Maybe you are dark-skinned, and you always find yourself avoiding the sun or using products that are supposed to make your skin look lighter. Perhaps you are one of those women who change the way you speak whenever you have a job interview, when you are on the phone, or when you first meet people. Maybe you have curly/ wavy/kinky hair, and you spend hours straightening it in the morning; you get your hair relaxed all the time, or you get the Brazilian Blowout done on your hair in order to keep it straight. Perhaps you have considered having plastic surgery (or you have already done it) so that you can have more of a rounded and voluptuous bottom or a slimmer/less bumpy nose. Maybe you wear blue contact lenses, and you claim they are just fashion lenses, yet deep down you wish you had blue eyes. Perhaps you always wear a blonde weave, or you dye your hair a different color from your natural one all the time because you feel that it's a better hair color for you. Or maybe you wear preppy-style clothing because you feel that it's a cleaner and more acceptable look. Whatever it is that you do, you may be doing it because you are trying to look like someone else.

To add to the pressure to fit the ideal standard set by who knows whom (possibly by those in power or majority) , there are the stereotypes that people have of each other across and within each ethnic group to which we are *supposed* to adhere. Whatever race you are, there is a notion that you should act, sound, and look like everyone in your race, and you must all have the same preferences. If you go beyond those boundaries, people label you with terms such as *oreo* or *coconut*, or your parents/peers/society scold you because you are not "sticking to your roots."

For example, you are black and you happen to like Japanese street fashion; you are white and you cannot get enough of West African music (Soukous, Makossa, etc.), or you are Asian, and you love Latin Ballroom, but people always try to get you to fancy what "your own kind" is supposed to fancy, so you end up feeling like a misfit. Fortunately for you, my sister, you are not *supposed* to conform to what anybody says you should.

When God created you, he never meant for you to conform to a standard of how everyone should look, act, or sound. If we were all the same, then none of us would be like God. What a shame that would be because God is the most diverse being in the entire universe. It is true. Look at his creation. It is an expression of who he is. Think about the many types of trees that exist, for example. There are oak trees, sycamore trees, pine trees, peach trees, just to name a few. These are all trees, but they are different. How about all the animals in the world? Some live on land and others in the sea. There are fish, whales, lizards, birds, cats, flies, bears, squirrels, horses, and millions of other species. These are all animals, but they are different and unique, and within each species, there are varieties to their appearance and behaviors. You never see them fighting to be like another type of animal or striving to conform to how they think they are supposed to be. They just are. For example, not once has a Chihuahua tried to be a bulldog or vice versa. Animals do what they do best without the pressure to fit a mold, and you need to do the same because you are also God's unique creation.

Stop trying to be someone else. Be proud of who *you* are. Whatever race/ethnicity you are, that is how God chose for you to represent him. If God looked one particular way, John would not have had such a hard time describing him. He had the privilege of seeing Jesus face to face, and he found it extremely difficult to describe our Savior (see Revelation 1:12–18). He kept on using similes to describe Jesus' features, but one thing is certain from his attempt to describe him: God is drop-dead gorgeous, absolutely stunning, magnificent in every way imaginable and more. He is *fi- iine!* And the best part is *you* are made in his image (see Genesis 1:26). Our Lord took a part of himself and inserted it into the body he gave you to use. You are beautiful just as you are because you look like your Father. God is captivated by your beauty. When he looks at you, he cannot help but be awe-struck by how gorgeous you are. My sister, *you* are "fearfully and wonderfully made" (Psalm 139:14).

Rejection

Rejection stings! We have all experienced it and will continue to experience it. You could get a rejection letter from a university or job you really want. It could be a guy who ends a relationship with you or who rejects your advances because he is not interested in you. Your friends could turn their backs on you. You could be refused government aide. Your mother or father or both parents may have left you or disowned you; if you are adopted, you may feel rejected by your birth parents. Whichever way you experience it, rejection may leave you feeling unloved, unwanted, insignificant, disheartened, or useless. All sorts of feelings arise from being rejected, and if those feelings are left unresolved, they could be detrimental to your self-image.

I do not know what kind of rejection you have experienced, but I know that you are in good company. Jesus understands exactly how you feel, and he wants to comfort and encourage you because he also experienced rejection when he was on earth. Have you ever been rejected by people with whom you grew up, people from your hometown? How about your friends—have any of them ever stabbed you in the back? Or maybe you had a best friend who pretended that she did not know you when you needed her the most. Have you ever had a parent reject you? The good news is - you are not alone.

You can turn to your Savior for comfort because he, too, was rejected by his hometown. If you look at Jesus' ministry, he hardly did any miracles in Nazareth because people said things such as, "Isn't this Mary's son?" (Mark 6:3) In other words, they were saying, "We have known that Jesus since he was a kid; he is nothing special." You could be getting the same message from people in your hometown, but do not worry because Jesus was and is amazing, and so are you!

Or perhaps you have been stabbed in the back by a friend. If so, you can turn to Jesus for comfort because he was also stabbed in the back by one of his friends. Judas betrayed Jesus with a kiss; something shared between friends in that culture. Judging from Jesus' reaction, "You betray the Son of Man with a kiss?" (Luke 22:48 NLT), his heart was in pain. Maybe your friend(s) used something shared to betray you, and now you are hurt and in deep sorrow. Let Jesus console you; he can help.

As for a friend pretending not to know you, you can turn to the Lord because he also had a friend who pretended not to know him at a crucial time in his life. Do you remember when Peter rejected Jesus three times before the cock crowed? Jesus must have been devastated when he heard one of his closest friends disowned him in public. You have been devastated too, and Jesus wants to soothe your soul. He has been where you are right now.

Jesus understands exactly how you feel. He knows the pain associated with any kind of rejection you have faced or that you will face because he has felt that pain too. Every single human experience came upon him when he was beaten and crucified (Isaiah 53:5), that's why he asked his Daddy if he could avoid going through the crucifixion (Luke 22:42). He knows where it hurts, and he truly empathizes with you. He is the only one who can fully comprehend whatever feelings you have from being rejected, and he is waiting for you to call on him for help. He says, "Come to me, all who are weary and heavy-laden, and I will give you rest" (Matthew 11:28 NASB). He longs to comfort you. Go to him and let him replace your pain with his peace, love, and joy.

Location

The world is big. There are many countries in it and even more people. Some people and places are known more than others, and there are many people who feel disadvantaged because of where they live. Perhaps you are one of those people. Maybe you come from a town where there are no big opportunities to move your life towards success and you feel stuck. You could be living in an impoverished nation/city/neighborhood and you cannot think of any way to get yourself out of your situation, so you feel trapped. Perhaps you live in one of the better places, but you are not where you would like to be in life. You feel you have no control over your destiny, even though on the outside it looks as if you have it made. Take heart, sister, because if you are joined together with the Holy Spirit, you are not bound by your location or circumstances in this world.

God is not limited by time, space, location, situations, or the ideas of this world. He has his own ways of doing business, and his ways are good. Never let where you come from determine who you are or who you will be. Jesus didn't. Nathanael's (one of the disciples) initial response when he was told about Jesus and that he came from Nazareth was not, "Oh, how wonderful! The Messiah is here!" Instead, he opened his big mouth and said, "Can anything good come from there?" (John 1:46) Need I remind you that Jesus came from a poor family that had its share of trouble? At a very young age (he was at most two years old), his family had to escape a king bent on killing him. He lived in Egypt as a refugee through some of his childhood, and then he had to leave again. That is how he ended up in an obscure town called Nazareth from where, according to Big Mouth Nate, nothing good came. (Read Matthew 2 for more about Jesus' childhood).

Nevertheless, that did not faze Jesus because he knew who he was. He refused to be defined by people's opinion of his background and situation, and he treated others with the same respect. Jesus never defined people by their circumstances or background, but by who they were in God's eyes. He saw potential where others saw failure.

One example, Matthew was a tax collector. So many people, especially the Pharisees, looked down on him. But Jesus did not; he saw a disciple. The woman at the well was a Samaritan, a person with whom a Jewish person would never associate. On top of that, she was a woman, and men in Jesus' culture did not regard women highly. To her fellow Samaritans, she was a whore, but Jesus saw past her background, gender, and situation; he saw an evangelist.

Nicodemus had it made. Firstly, he was a Jew. Secondly, he was a Jew who had the best education that any Jew could acquire; he was well versed in the Law. Finally, he was a Pharisee and a member of the Sanhedrin. He was a very important person, but Jesus saw past that and into an aching heart. Nicodemus wanted more than his life could give him.

You may want more than your life can give you, too, and Jesus has many wonderful plans for you. He sees past your background and your situation. Your location or circumstances do not limit his great plans for you. When he looks at you, he does not see a small-town girl, an uneducated woman, a poor person, someone who has already reached her limit, or any negative way you view yourself. Instead, he sees you as a powerful and victorious woman with limitless possibilities. You can do all things through the one who gave his life for you, and he wants *that* to define who you are.

Chapter 7

Sex, Love, and Marriage

*The body is not meant for sexual immorality
but for the Lord, and the Lord for the body.
1 Corinthians 6:13*

Admit it. You were looking forward to reading this part of the book. Congratulations! You are just like many women out there who want to talk about sex, but for some reason, they think it is inappropriate to talk about, and God forbid, desire it. After all, a woman of integrity, a woman of character and right standing with God does not discuss or desire such things, right? That is only for loose women in the world who need to be saved so that they, too, can become the rigid, overworked, uninformed, and under-sexed women religion has said they should be.

Ladies, if you did not already know, talking about or desiring sex is not bad. It is normal, and women, especially single Christian women, should be informed about what God says about it if we are to honor him with our bodies. You have spent your entire life listening to what the world says about sex, but now it is time to open your Bible and ask God to guide you as you locate what *he* thinks about what he created. Yes, you read that correctly; God created sex. In Genesis 1:27 it says God created males and females in his image. Then in verse 28, he told them to "be fruitful and increase in number." In other words, he was saying have sex as much as you want so that there can be more of you on the planet. But before you get any ideas, he created Adam and Eve and made them husband and wife *before* they could "become one flesh" showing that sex is supposed to be between a man and his wife (Genesis 2:24).

That is just the beginning of what the Bible says about sex, but plenty of times, it is clear that sex is meant for married people. But you may be thinking, "I'm not married, so as a single woman what do I do with the desire I have for it?" The truth is, you may have already dealt with that desire, but perhaps not in the way God wants. You may have let your desire for sex lead you to sin. You may have committed fornication, which is sex outside of marriage. You may not have done the deed, but you may have masturbated while thinking all sorts of impure thoughts, dry humped, have been fondled, watched pornography, or to make yourself feel better you have thought, "It's only sex when it's vaginal or anal," so you have either given and/or gotten oral sex. These are all sexually immoral sins, no matter how you try to bend and twist them to make them okay.

It is essential that you abstain from your desire to sin sexually, for when you commit a sexually immoral sin, you sin against your own body. Your body was never "meant for sexual immorality, but for the Lord, and the Lord for your body" (1 Corinthians 6:13). Since your body was made for the Lord, take your desire for sex to him. Talk to Jesus about it! It may feel awkward at first, but you will become comfortable quickly once you realize that he already knows your thoughts and desires, so you might as well tell him. He knows you better than you know yourself, so go to him, and you will find out some extremely interesting truths about yourself, especially concerning this area. Talk to him; trust me, and I say this from experience, *you want* to hear what he has to say and show you.

    I know I am not mistaken when I say you want to experience romantic love; the kind of love that leads to marriage. Nevertheless, you may not care about getting married, but you still want love. There is something about it that no one is capable of understanding unless you look at it from God's perspective. God is love, and out of his love he created you. You were created to love and to serve him (Deuteronomy 10:12 NLT). Because he loves you, he looks forward to having an intimate relationship with you. I am not talking about a parent/child, friend to friend, or sibling type intimacy. The Lord wants all of that with you, but the most intimate kind of love is the one between lovers, and that is what he wants from you. He wants you to be passionately in love with him because that is how he feels about you. He wants you to see him as your boyfriend, your lover, your fiancé, your husband.

    Even though I have previously mentioned this, you may still be cringing at the thought of God being your lover. You are thinking, "Um, that doesn't sound right." Do yourself a favor and go read the book of Hosea in the Old Testament. God commanded the prophet Hosea to marry a prostitute because the children of Israel had committed "great harlotry by departing from the Lord" (Hosea 1: 2 NKJV). Later, God tells Hosea to take back his wife who had left him with the same love that God has for his people even though they look to other gods (Hosea 3: 1). In chapter 2:16, God says that his people will call him "my husband" and in verses 19-20, he says he will marry his people with righteousness, justice, loving kindness, and mercy. God shows himself as a faithful husband, even though his people continuously cheat on him and do not always love him. He loves his people as a husband loves his wife. In Isaiah 54:5, he calls himself your husband and your Redeemer. Jesus loves you, sister. He loves you as a lover, like that faithful husband, and he wants you to love him back with the same passion.

You may be wondering what any of this has to do with your getting married, but it has everything to do with it. You are called to love God above all else. You must love him more than you love yourself, your friends, your family, your job, your handbag, food, TV, everything. Psalm 37:4 says, "Take delight in the Lord, and he will give you the desires of your heart." Do you yearn for love, marriage? Then find your pleasure and enjoyment in the One who gave you those desires.

The problem is many of us are not willing to take delight in Jesus. We do not want to do the work it takes, but we still want all the rewards that come from the effort. Hebrews 11:6 clearly states that those who diligently seek the Lord are the ones who are rewarded, but we often prefer to listen only to the latter half of Psalm 37:4 and then become angry with God because we think he is not answering our prayers. Sister, many of God's promises come in "if . . . then" statements. They are conditional. The two verses above could be phrased like this: "If you take delight in the Lord, then he will give you the desires that he has placed in your heart." And "if you diligently seek the Lord, then you will be rewarded."

That means you do not just place demands on the Holy Spirit; you cooperate with him.

You may be thinking, "But I do seek the Lord. I take delight in him, so I don't understand why he isn't answering me." Be honest with yourself, are you really seeking God, or are you treating him like a vending machine? You think, "All I have to do is give God my time; I tell him what I want, then he gives it to me. And if he doesn't, I will kick, shake, and rattle him, maybe add a few tears, and he will bend to my will. "Perhaps some of your prayers sound something like this:

> Lord, I want a boyfriend. Why is it that **everyone** around me has one? Now half of my friends are married, but I'm still single, and it sucks. **Why won't you give me a boyfriend?** Why do you keep holding out on me? Don't you want me to be happy? Do you even love me? You say you love me, **but you never do anything for me!** *Sniff.*

That kind of prayer can apply to any area of life—your finances, your health, your relationships. But the common theme from this type of prayer is that your heart is not open to what God has to say. You are so consumed with what you want from God that you do not give him a chance to talk to you. And then, when you do not hear from him, you begin to doubt his love for you. You read your Bible and refuse to believe any of his promises, so you become angry with him because he will not respond to your demands.

For your information, God is not a vending machine. He is a being with feelings. He is a being who longs to be known, loved, and understood by his people, by you. He is more than willing to reveal himself to you. In fact, he already has, and he desires for you to discover him even more. Do you not want the same too? Do you not want people to *really* know you and understand you? How would you like it if people only came to you to get something from you and nothing else? Maybe in your quest for love, you have been in relationships in which the guy only took from you and never gave, but because of your desire to be known, you gave him money, your body, your car, or your time, yet he never gave you anything in return. Perhaps it was not a romantic relationship, but you have friends, family members, and others who keep on taking from you, but they never give anything in return. All they do is talk to you sweetly whenever they want something from you, and you let them take advantage of you because you want to make them happy. You do all of that hoping they will give you love, but they never do. That part of you that longs to be known, loved, and understood is never satisfied.

Let me tell you something, sister, God does not want that happening to him. You are trying to treat him as those people treat you, but he will not budge. Yes, he wants you to experience all of his blessings, but in order for you to experience them to the fullest, you have to get to know him. He wants you to believe in him first. He wants you to trust him completely. If he just gave you what you wanted when you asked for it, you would not be interested in loving him because you would have already gotten what you wanted. Jesus will not tolerate that kind of relationship. He did not die for you so you would ignore him. He is jealous for you. He will not let anything, or anyone be first in your life when he should be first. He longs for you to yearn for him as he yearns for you. He wants the two of you to have a deep and intimate relationship, and out of that will come the blessings you desire. But, of course, you prefer to seek after the blessings and not the One who gives them.

You may be worried that you will never get married because you think God is taking too long, so you have decided to help God find you a mate. You walk into a church service, and the first thing you do is look for the single men. Maybe you have joined the singles' ministry. You are immediately attracted to the guy who raises his hands during worship and who tells you about the mission trip he has done and how he is so excited to serve the Lord. As he continues to talk to you, you begin to daydream about the beautiful babies you will have with him. As the two of you get to know each other, he begins to court you, and you happily let him because now you have found the right man for you. You cannot stop thanking God for finally coming through for you. But then the guy breaks up with you right before you thought he was going to propose, and you are devastated.

Perhaps you date someone who is absolutely dangerous for you. You still have many issues that God needs to heal, but you look for healing through a relationship with a man. You think having a boyfriend and eventually getting married to him will solve your problems. You see that man as your savior, but he is also broken and needs Jesus. You both fool yourselves into thinking you are meant for each other, and you vow to have a relationship built on Christ, even though your individual lives are not built on him. As a result, you always find yourself having sex with him, having all kinds of naughty thoughts about him, sexting him, masturbating to his voice on the phone, or you 69 each other frequently. Maybe you get sucked into any addictions he has all in the name of love, or your addictions worsen.

You may hunt for a relationship, and not once do you think to let God be involved in the way he needs to be involved. You date a guy and hesitantly ask God if he is "the one." You hear the answer you want to hear because you are not truly open to God's opinion. Maybe you foolishly go after a married man because you believe he is the right man for you. Or in your desperation, you compromise and date someone who is not a Christian because you believe you are going to change him and lead him to Christ. You do it because you are convinced that the two of you are perfect for each other. He just needs to become a Christian and you are set; you can get married.

Dear sister, I used to be on that quest just as you are until I eventually realized how worthless it was, and you need that revelation as well. God does not need you to help him find a husband for you. Besides, he already has one for you and *it is not your job to locate him.* He will come to you. When it is time for you to get married, he will show up. It's true. Genesis 2:24 says, "A man will leave his father and mother and be united to his wife." Nowhere in that verse does it say, "And a woman will go bonkers looking for a husband until finally, after many failed relationships or vain attempts at being in a relationship, she will be united to him." God *foreknew* that you wanted to get married before he created the world, so he *fore-found* you a husband so that you would not have to look for him. Therefore, relax, sister. Stop the agonizing search and find your joy in the Lord.

Unwanted Attention – A Courtship Story

Being led by the Holy Spirit is so much fun, and it's filled with adventure. I have enjoyed all my conversations with him, especially the ones about men. Regardless, there are times when he leads me into situations that I am not so fond of. In 2014, an acquaintance of mine, Charlotte (not her real name), tried to hook me up with one of her friends. I don't like to be set up, so my immediate response was, no, but Daddy told me that even though I was not going to like him, I should give the boy a chance. With my father's approval, I went ahead and told Charlotte to give him my phone number. BIG MISTAKE! The moment this boy got my number, he called my phone several times. When I didn't answer any of his calls, he complained to Charlotte that I wasn't responding. She told him I was at work. We finally spoke after I finished work, but I already saw signs of trouble. The next day, after another set of missed calls from him, we spoke again, and he accused me of being coy. In essence, he wanted me to make it easy for him to be with me and he didn't appreciate having to work for my attention. He also insulted me several times while we spoke. I wished he had never gotten my number.

After that conversation with him, I went to Charlotte's house, and when he found out from her that I was there, he left work early so he could meet me. I dreaded the idea of seeing him face to face. When he arrived, I was absolutely appalled by what I witnessed. Not only was he incredibly unattractive, but he was replete with lust and was not ashamed of it. During his entire impromptu visit, that despicable beast looked me up and down like a piece of meat at the butcher. Also, he continually looked for excuses to touch me, and after several attempts to keep his roaming hands away from my body, I forcefully told him not to touch me.

Charlotte decided he should take us to the grocery store. She needed to get some personal items and some food for her nephews. To my chagrin, she made me sit with him in the front, and the lad nearly crashed the car because he couldn't keep his eyes on the road but carried on eyeing me with that sickening hunger for sex. When we got out of the car and walked into the store, he purposely lingered behind me so he could get a better view of my backside. I could feel his eyes feasting on my bum, and I grew even more disgusted of him when he walked up beside me with a satisfied grin on his face. I felt like vomiting. I had never been so disrespected and felt so violated in my life.

He decided to go back to work and Charlotte and I walked back to her place. I expressed my anger at her for trying to set me up with someone with such a terrible character, but since he was her friend, I didn't tell her the full extent of my disapproval. When we arrived at her house, I lay on her bed and spent some time with the Holy Spirit. I told him how unhappy I was with him for putting me through this situation. He told me to end everything. The boy called me soon afterward and asked when I would see him again. I let him know that his feel-

ings for me were not mutual and I hadn't the desire to ever see him again. He pleaded with me to give him another chance and I tersely refused and hung up. He sent a text to Charlotte and told her I had been cold-hearted. I didn't care.

To this day, I don't know why God led me through this atrocious ordeal except to teach you about it. As you can see, this is another example of what can happen if you don't listen to Holy Spirit's leadership. In my case, he had already informed me that I wouldn't like this boy. Normally, I would not have followed through with giving him my number, but because God had told me to give it to him, I obliged. I believe he did that in order for you and me to clearly see the results of going on "getting to know you" dates without God's wisdom and knowledge on the matter. Many of you most likely don't consult God before talking to a guy and you end up in situations like the one I was in. Save yourself the trouble of meeting useless men and follow his guidance.

Chapter 8

Let Him In

*Here I am! I stand at the door and knock.
If anyone hears my voice and
opens the door, I will come in.
Revelation 3:20*

"Is this chick for real? She's asking us to be single and be happy about it! She's crazy; I need a man by my side."

Yes, you have that absolutely correct. You need a Man by your side; that Man is Jesus. Yes, I am asking you to be single and to enjoy it. And yes, I *am* a wee bit off-kilter. There is nothing wrong with being single because that is the time you can be completely focused on God and his kingdom. As a single woman, you do not have the major commitments of maintaining a household (catering to your husband, children, in-laws, etc.) This is the best time for you to fully delve into what he is doing in the world. (I understand that some of you have children or other life circumstances that you feel may hinder your destiny, but God has many sweet surprises in store for you. Do not let your circumstances limit the endless possibilities of your very bright future.) You can go wherever he wants you to go when he says you should go.

There is nothing holding you back. What a wonderful opportunity you have to be included in his glorious plans!

This is the time when Jesus wants to teach you how to love him. He wants you to fall *head over heels* in love with him because only then can you know how to love the man for whom you keep searching. He wants to be first in your life. He wants you to have complete trust and confidence in him and to fully depend on him for everything. He is your life source, and that is why he is your Savior. Many of you are looking for a boyfriend/husband so you can have someone on whom to depend, a knight in shining armor, but guess what? The man you are looking for also wants what you want. How, then, is your relationship going to be strong if both you and your husband are depending on each other for life support? That is a train wreck waiting to happen because eventually, you will both realize that you are mere mortals, and you cannot be each other's saviors.

All you need is Jesus. He is your Savior. He wants to teach you how to live the kind of life that he lived while he was on earth; a life filled with the supernatural. He has many wondrous signs to show you. He wants you to be a woman who has great faith, a powerful woman of God who casts out devils, heals the sick, speaks in tongues, rebukes storms, raises the dead, and walks by faith and not by sight (Matthew 10:8; 15:28–30, Mark 16:17-18, Luke 8:24, 2 Corinthians 5:7 KJV). He wants you to be a woman who believes God about anything and everything, who reigns in life, and who does not fear (Mark 9:23, Romans 5:17, 2 Timothy 1:7 KJV). He wants you to experience all of this *before* you get married. Do you not want the same? Do you not want to reign in life?

You belong to *the* royal family. You are the daughter of the Most High. You are the child of the Creator of the universe. You are a princess. The man you want is a prince in the Father's kingdom. You rule over "all the power of the enemy" and "over all the earth" because you have the Almighty God living inside of you, and you have complete access to him (Luke 10:19, Genesis 1:26). As a believer, you have been given authority by Jesus to rule, to use his supernatural power. Imagine yourself reigning over everything in life – your relationships, your finances, your emotions (especially any fears), your daily routine, your job, unruly bosses and co-workers, difficult subjects at school, your time, your health, your sleep. God wants you to rule, ladies! He wants you to be a powerful and fearless woman of God while you are still single, and he wants your husband to be a powerful and fearless man of God while he is still single so that when the two of you are made one, you will do even more marvelous works for Him. Your single years are the years Jesus wants to use to build your faith in a great way. He wants to make it so forceful that when you and your husband get married, there will be an explosion of God's power and might in your lives.

However, you cannot do any of this if you continue to chase after everything and everyone but God. Jesus wants you to be completely devoted to him if you are going to reign in life. When you received your salvation, you died to yourself. You made Jesus Lord over your life, meaning you do what he wants you to do. You will live a more victorious life if you do his will because his will for your life is good. You serve a good God, ladies. He loves you deeply and wants you to love him the same way. He wants you to be *in love* with him. How can you resist falling in love with the Man who died for you so that you would not have to? How can you resist falling in love with the Man who heals all your pain and has completely freed you from your guilty conscience? How can you resist being in love with the Man who longs for you to experience his supernatural power, peace, love, joy, and prosperity?

All you have to do to experience Jesus' blessings is to spend time with him. That's it. Get to know him. Talk to him every day. Be authentic about everything: if you are angry with him, shout at him. If you had a bad day at work, tell him. If you do not like your siblings, tell him. If you are feeling frustrated, tell him. If you are feeling tempted, tell him. He is there for you, and that is why his Holy Spirit lives in you. Include him in everything you do. Sing praises to him. Write a poem for him. Paint or draw a picture for him. Go shopping with him. Whatever thing you like, do it for him and with him. Read your Bible every day and believe all the wonderful promises in his Word. Ask him to teach you how to be in love with him. I did, and ever since I fell in love with him, my faith has gotten much stronger. Your faith can and will get stronger too. He holds back nothing from you, so let him take over your life. Let him consume you with his love, and you will be amazed at the victorious life you will live. Let him in. He is waiting.

Conclusion

An unmarried woman or virgin is concerned about the Lord's affairs: Her aim is to be devoted to the Lord in both body and spirit.
1 Corinthians 7:34

I know you may be finding it difficult to let Jesus take over your life, especially where dating is concerned. You have believed the lie that says singleness is not something to be desired. Society tells you that it is not okay to be single. It tells you that you find your identity, among other things, in romantic relationships. Child of God, it is essential that you stop looking for wholeness in other people and look to your Maker for your identity. Let Jesus define who you are. As you spend time with him, he will begin to show you exactly who you are, and you will find total satisfaction. You will be completely gratified and so filled with his love that you will get to a point where you will not care to have a boyfriend. Believe me; it is possible.

I would like to share two stories of women I know who have devoted their lives to loving God. They both have been influential in my life, and I hope that their stories will inspire you to consider giving your heart to Jesus where your love life is concerned.

From One Single Woman to Another

Katie Oliver, a dear friend of mine.

"I never really know how to tell a story. When in doubt, I just share in chronological order what I feel is relevant. I'll begin with me as a child. I have always been called 'boy crazy'. From the time I was young, I have had a deep desire to be a wife and mom someday. As a teenager, I found myself feeling unattractive, uninteresting, and maybe slightly picky. I was having zero luck in the guy department, so I prayed, 'Lord, I stink at this. I have horrible taste in men, and I am awkward. I place my romance into your hands for you are wiser and see things more clearly than I do. You will write my love story better than I can.'

Even though I placed my romance into God's hands, I have remained boy crazy. However, I celebrate my singleness and the fact that I have never settled. I enjoy dating, but the majority of men I have met have been 'dead end guys'; guys who were not a right fit and ended up being just a friend or a bad memory. Still, the desire to find love and be married rests in my heart. When I convince myself that something is wrong with me, God reminds me that I placed my story into His hands. He tells me that relationships have not worked out because none have been right for me. With these words, I inhale, exhale, trust God, and rejoice in His comfort and His presence.

Singleness has been a rollercoaster ride both emotionally and physically. It is easy to feel blessed by the freedom at times, and other days, there's a weight of loneliness upon me. In 2013, a significant turning point happened to me. I was months from uprooting and moving from Texas to Tennessee to follow where I felt God was leading me. While sitting on the edge of a friend's swimming pool, I felt God ask, 'If I were to give you heaven or a husband right now which would you choose?' To my surprise, without hesitation, I answered, 'Give me heaven.' That night, it sank in for me that God is my top priority and to be with Him is my ultimate goal. There lingers in my spirit a sense that God has a husband for me, and I rest in that sense and prayerfully interact with men.

In August 2015, some friends and I took a weekend to trip to Gatlinburg. We had a wonderful time hiking, zip lining, facing fears, trying new things, eating good food, and resting. Our drive back home took us down winding tree-lined roads. As I rode in the passenger seat, I soaked in the beauty and replayed the weekend's events in my mind. My thoughts turned, and I started a mental conversation with my husband. In thought, I said to him, 'I wish you were here. I wish you were by my side seeing all of this and having these adventures with me. I wish you were here, but I will not be still as I wait for you. I will live my life and have good times and not hold back from making memories; no matter how much I wish you were here.'

Another conversation like this took place a couple of months after I had bought my house. As my home *was becoming more and more familiar, there were times I was overwhelmed with the need to fix things, to keep the lawn mowed, and to make tough decisions by myself. I celebrate the fact that I have a house; I often feel empowered that I bought a house, but there are times when I am somewhat sad that it's all on me. One of those times I said to my husband, 'I wish you were here. I feel things would be easier if you were here. Still, I celebrate this house and this time of my life. I will continue living and will not be still even as I wish you were here.'*

Though there are hard days of loneliness, I live with a full heart and full faith that God is with me. He knows the desires of our hearts and He knows what is best for us. I rest in the security of His presence and the knowledge of how He loves and provides what is best for us. I have security in my relationship with Him, and I know I will be happy even if marriage is not in my future. He is a good, good Father. Not separate from us for even a second but by our side in every moment."

Worth the Wait: From Singleness to Marriage

Sarah Stewart is a lady I met when I was a student at Texas A&M University. She was one of the staff members at my church. When we met, she had been single for 10 years with no hope of ever finding a husband in a college town. Four years later, I got the privilege to attend her wedding to a wonderful man and now father to her children, Andrew Stewart. He too had been wrestling with singleness for several years, but God brought them together in a delightful way. Here is Sarah's story:

*

"When I was younger, I was boy crazy. I had many guy friends, and I liked being playful with them. I was aware of boys, and I wanted their attention, so I was that girl who had many boyfriends in sixth grade. However, when puberty hit in middle school, I became more aware that boys wanted sex from girls, and I was afraid. So, from middle school and throughout high school I didn't have boyfriends. There were many boys I liked, but nothing came out of that.

In high school, I experienced two major heartbreaks that caused me to make the vow that I was never going to love a man again. As a result, I wanted to use men before they could use me so that I would not get hurt again. There were still many guys I liked, but I had stopped giving my heart to any of them.

At 20 years old, I started following Jesus. Two years leading up to this point, I had been involved in highly sexual relationships, but I neither dated nor had any *boyfriends. Following my salvation, I moved to College Station, TX where I was a student at Texas A&M University. One of the guys I had dated in high school also attended A&M. He and I quickly rekindled and got involved sexually the first night we saw each other. That night, while in bed with him, I suddenly felt God's presence in the room. I felt that what I was doing was impure and God was watching me. He was seeing it all. I was so struck by this sudden realization that I made the guy leave, and I said out loud that I was done with boys. Little did I know that God would take what I said seriously for 13 years.*

Throughout my time as a student and for several years serving at my local church as a missionary to college students, I was single, and it wasn't easy. Even though I had said I was done with boys, I still longed for a companion. There were many guys whom I liked, and I still wanted male attention, but no boys came in my direction. I watched with sadness (and sometimes bitterness) as all my peers found the love of their lives and got married. One by one they all got married and I felt alone and disheartened because I was only around college students. I kept on wondering when I was going to find someone who was my age in a college town.

Although I felt that I was on a lonely path of singleness, God restored that vow of distrust that I had made back in high school. Jesus healed and restored me, and I embraced the truth that I could love a man and that I didn't have to fear being hurt. Despite this restoration,

I found it to be a bittersweet healing because my heart opened to the possibility of love and marriage. My boy crazy days came back, and I found myself liking many guys. There was a period after I had declared that I was done with boys in which I didn't really think about guys at all, and instead, pursued the Lord, but those days were over, and feelings of confusion came over me. There were no men who were pursuing me at all, and I wondered if something was wrong with me. I struggled to believe the truth that nothing was wrong with me. God was my Father and he had the perfect timing for all things.

I learned many lessons during those thirteen years that I was single. Through the tears, the phone calls to friends, the encouraging words that I read in my Bible, and the many journal entries in which I continually gave my heart to God and cried out to him about the boys I liked who didn't reciprocate my feelings, I truly matured into a woman who was wholeheartedly devoted to Jesus.

One of the first lessons God taught me was to trust him with my love life. I was afraid to give him that part of my life. I thought that if I did, he was going to give me a man who only had a good personality and no physical features I found enticing. Somehow, I believed the lie that God didn't care about that, so I thought if I surrendered to him, he would give me a man I wasn't attracted to so that I would learn a lesson about marriage. I also thought that he would say, 'Okay, great! I'm glad you're content. Now you can stay single the rest of your life!' I often had to revisit that statement and challenge it with the notion that God had the best plan for me, and if he wants me to be single my whole life, then he knows best. However, that notion came through tears, prayer, and friends who also prayed and encouraged me.

The biggest lesson he taught me was that his love, his delight in me, and his attention were far better than a man's attention. I learned that I didn't have to fear his love or be ashamed of it, so I opened my heart wide to his love and his delight, and I let myself be immersed in his affection. I also got to experience how a healthy marriage and family looked through the many friends I made in my church. I came from a very broken home, so I appreciated the opportunity given to me to observe and be loved by many healthy families in my church.

Since I was single with no suitors or anything holding me down, I got to go on many adventures. I traveled around the world on mission trips and I had more time available to fully exercise my gifts and strengths. I was able to use them in the areas where they fit best, both in the church and in the world. Now, as a married woman with two sons, I no longer have ample time to travel and practice my gifts to a full extent, so I am grateful for the time that I got to do that.

Lastly, I learned how to take care of myself in a loving community of believers as well as in my own time. I got to really understand how to love myself well and

CONCLUSION

how to function in a ministry. This one came with some trial and error, but it was a lesson I really needed to learn before marriage because now I know how to love my husband and children with a heart that has been restored and shaped into a wife, mother, and best friend to many.

My sister, Katie, is 38 and still single. It has been 15 long years for her, but she is really trusting God for her life partner. She has gone on a few dates here and there, but nothing has materialized from them. She and I share the struggles I faced with singleness. She has her bouts of discontentment and distrust of God just as I did, but she is truly an overcomer. Instead of lagging and helplessly waiting for a man to come to her rescue like a damsel in distress, she's making the most of her single years. I always encourage her to wait because I feel that there's someone there for her. She just has to wait as I waited. And in the waiting, she is asking the Lord to help her leave a legacy of joy on the earth whether she ends up married or not. I know for single women it is hard to fight the temptation to jump into a relationship when substandard men come along, but I always encourage her not to lose heart and wait for the man God has for her. If I hadn't waited for my husband, I would have missed out on a great man who is compatible with me in so many ways. When I look back to my single years, I can wholeheartedly say that I do not regret them. I find it easier to say now that I'm on the other side of singlehood, but I am truly satisfied with the fact that I waited. So, ladies, I encourage you to wait well. Wait for the man God has designed for you. He will be worth the wait."

*

Sarah and Andy had been friends before they started dating. Sarah found this particularly sweet because she had always wanted to marry her best friend. She had been attracted to Andy ever since she met him, but she never thought he was an option for her because he's younger than her. So, when she realized that they both liked each other, she couldn't believe she liked a guy who actually liked her back. Before dating, they sought God's wisdom. Four months later, God approved them, and they decided to date. Within a year and a half, they got married. It had been made apparent to both of them that they were meant for marriage, so there was no use in having a long courtship. It has been seven years since their marriage, and they are still awestruck with wonder at how God brought them together.

CONCLUSION

There is always a good purpose to everything God does, so trust his ways. Rely on his love, his power, and his guidance. He loves you and always wants you to be fully prepared for any challenge in life, so let him guide you. Depend on him. Trust him. Expect great things from him. Hallelujah!

A Prayer for you by Sarah Stewart

Sarah prayed for me after I interviewed her, and I wanted to share the prayer with you as it applies to all women:

Father, I ask that you would anoint Tatenda in her book writing and I pray that it would get in the hands of so many women who need hope, and who need to wait on your best. I pray that there would be a mighty force of women in this generation who will trust you, who will be courageous, who will be mighty warriors, God, to conquer sin and brokenness in this world, and who will be able to find awesome men of God who have stepped up and want to take this time to wage war alongside them in the Kingdom. God, I ask that you give _____

(write your name) hope in her heart and give her grace and strength to wait well. That's exactly what we want, Lord. We don't want to just wait. We want to wait well. So, let us wait well. Let us not wait with discontentment and grumbling, hopelessness, bitterness, unforgiveness, or any other negative emotion. We pray that you would uproot any of these negative emotions from our hearts and that we would wait well no matter what season we're in. I pray that for_____

(write your name). We pray for the community around her; that you would give her great friendships and great relationships and that the husband you intend for her will find her soon, if you so desire, Lord. And if she is to wait longer for him, then I pray that she'll be able to be loved by you and comforted, and be full of life and joy. We thank you so much in Jesus' name. Amen.

The Divine Dance

I am sitting to the side of the dance floor. I hear the music,
but it doesn't move me.
I don't belong here – me in my faded t-shirt
and ripped jeans.

I don't belong here, in this sparkling, shimmering place
where the lights are a deep blue, the ceiling is filled with
twinkling stars, and the dancers swirl effortlessly
with their partners.
Their partners. Everyone has one. Everyone but me.

So why am I even here? Why is partnerless,
ragged me even here?

Did I just decide to come? Did someone invite me? I can't
remember. And at this point, I don't even care.
That's it. I'm done. On the outside looking in isn't
doing me any good.

But as I get up to leave, I see a proffered hand. His hand.

The hand of the one who invited me to come.
I remember now.

I got an invitation from the King of Kings, and now
He is asking me to dance.

I feel unworthy, unclean, out of place in the
midst of such beauty.

I start to pull away, but He whispers in my ear,

HEAD OVER HEELS

"Dance with me."

Slowly, warily, I let myself be led through the paces of the waltz, ready to pull away at any moment, yet longing for the embrace. Looking up into His soft, caring eyes, I melt into the swaying rhythm. My world is no longer me, but we. I have begun letting go of myself.

Suddenly, I feel the presence of two others.

A Father, safe and protecting. A Spirit, warm and comforting.

The overwhelming love of the triune God supports me as I close my eyes, tilt back my head, and emit the clearest laugh of pure joy I have ever heard.

I can hardly believe it was me.

My feet no longer touch the floor, while my taffeta skirt floats around my snow-white shoes.

My white glove rests on my Partner's shoulder.

I am no longer mine, but His.

Gone are my grungy representations of self.

I am clothed in His righteousness, transformed by Love. Nothing matters now but dancing with my Father, my Counselor, and my Prince of Peace.

I am still awaiting the day when another man will join the dance.

Yet even then, the waltz will remain the same.

And until that day and far beyond, may I passionately pursue my Partner in this divine dance.

By Bethany Dunn

Poetchick4jesus.wordpress.com

Acknowledgments

It is amazing how far I have come throughout my Christian journey, and I know I would not be where I am now if it were not for the key people in my life. I want to thank the pastors at A&M Christian Fellowship in Bryan, Texas, for their hearts to reach out to college students. The four years I attended your church were essential to the inquisitive nature I have adopted in the past few years. Andrew Stewart, you were an awesome leader as well, and I will never forget how you also encouraged me to always read my Bible and verify that what you taught the home group was truth from the Word.

Macy Gonzalez, I love you and your beautiful red hair. Thank you for your obedience to the Lord and leading the session at the women's retreat in 2010. Because of you, I was finally able to be set free from the guilt and shame of my secret sin, and that allowed God to move my faith to where it is today. You are awesome!

Amy Hamm and Christina Martinez, I am very glad you were with me in Macy's session at the retreat. Thank you for your support when I confessed my problems. I am also grateful for your willingness to confess yours as well. I would have never been able to share my complete testimony if I had not shared it with you then.

Whitney Booth, your husband and your sons are lucky to have you in their lives. You are an amazing woman, and I thank you for sharing the vision God gave you about my future. It has kept me sane in times when I had doubted that I am walking in God's will for my life, especially when he told me to write this book.

Tyrone Johnson and Kelly Holmes, worship leader and member at Chase Oaks Church in Plano, Texas, I express my deepest gratitude to the two of you for counseling me at a time when I thought my life was over. I am also grateful to the former Pastoral Care Pastor, Steve McPherson, for encouraging me to pursue God's will for my life.

Pastor Fungayi, I am grateful for the Ladies of Purpose Conference you organized in the summer of 2012 because it was there that I found out what God's plan was for this season of my life. This book would not exist if I had not "fanned into flame the gift of God."

Kate Oliver, thank you for helping me proofread my manuscript. You are an awesome friend, and may God bless you as you continue to trust his guidance in your art career.

Bethany Dunn, to this day, I am in awe of the fact that you wrote "The Divine Dance" less than a year after I wrote my manuscript, yet we only met in 2018. Thank you for letting

ACKNOWLEDGMENTS

me add it to the book! I feel like the book is more complete now; thanks to your poem.

Mary Hollingsworth, author/speaker/publishing coach, I also thank you for editing my first manuscript. Your professional input helped me greatly.

Jesus, my Redeemer, my Lord, there are no words that can wholly describe how I feel about you. I am both humbled and honored that you have chosen me to minister to your daughters, and I am excited about how you are going to touch the lives of the women who will read this book. May it bring you more glory and honor forever!

With love,
Tatenda

P.S. I thank everyone else who has prayed for me or encouraged me in any way. May God bless you bountifully.

About the Author

Tatenda Dune was born in Harare, Zimbabwe, and moved to the United States when she was eleven. Currently, she lives in Dallas, TX and is part of the apostolic equipping center, Storehouse Dallas, a house of prayer that focuses on accessing heaven so that the earth can be transformed by Jesus' power and love.

In her leisure time, Tatenda enjoys singing, knitting, playing guitar, dancing, reading, and swimming. She also looks forward to helping in any way she can with Refuge City, a ministry dedicated to funding and providing homes of refuge to domestic victims of sexual exploitation and/or sexual human trafficking to children and women in the Dallas/Fort Worth. She holds a Bachelor of Arts degree in Psychology from Texas A&M University in College Station, TX.

Journal

What is God saying to you?

HEAD OVER HEELS

www.ingramcontent.com/pod-product-compliance
Lightning Source LLC
Chambersburg PA
CBHW020702300426
44112CB00007B/486